Santa Line-Up

by MizFitz

Leisure Arts · Maumelle Arkansas

Table of Contents

Production Team: Writer - Merrilee Gasaway; Senior Artist - Diana Sanders; Artist - Karen F. Allbright; and Photo Stylist - Cassie Newsome.

Some cover items made by Mary Kennemur.

We have made every effort to ensure that these instructions are accurate and complete. We cannot, however, be responsible for human error, typographical mistakes, or variations in individual work.

Made in U.S.A.

Special Project!

CHRISTMAS TREE HOLDER

Make your Christmas tree holder something special with a circle of all eight Santas. Just follow the instructions included with each Santa to stitch and assemble your Santas. Then, refer to Joining the Line-up on pg. 26 to hinge them together. Place a 10"h by 12" dia. clay pot in the center of the circle. We painted our pot metallic gold for a little added glitter.

Special Project!

KINDLING KEEPER

Add country charm to your fireplace. Simply follow the instructions on pg. 5 to stitch and assemble Country Santa. Attach your Santa to a 12"w x 12"h x 8"d basket to hold your kindling.

COUNTRY SANTA

Size: 5 1/2"w x 12 3/4"h

Supplies: Worsted weight yarn, white DMC Embroidery Floss, and Rainbow Gallery metallic gold yarn for 7 mesh (refer to color keys); two 10 1/2" x 13 1/2" sheets of clear 7 mesh plastic canvas; #16 tapestry needle; one 3" x 10" white foam board rectangle; two 12mm moveable eyes; four green buttons; powder blush; and craft glue.

Instructions:

You will need to refer to the photo when assembling your Santa.

1. Follow charts to cut and stitch Santa pieces, working backstitches, French knots, and Turkey loops last and leaving shaded areas unworked.
2. Tack Eyebrows, Nose, top edge of Mustache, and Shirt Trim to Front. Glue eyes and buttons to Front.
3. Tack Bird #1 and one Bird #2 to Tree; tack Tree to Arms. Tack Arms to Front.
4. Tack Buckle to Belt; tack Belt to Front. Tack Belt Loops to Front over Belt.
5. Tack Hatchet to Front; tack Hatchet Loop to Front over Hatchet.
6. Tack remaining Bird #2 to Cuffs; tack Cuffs and Bird #2 to Front.
7. Matching ✖'s, work stitches in green shaded areas through three layers of canvas to join Beard to Front and Back.
8. Matching ★'s, tack top of Shoes to Front. Place foam board rectangle between Front and Back. Working stitches in blue shaded area and stitching through three layers of canvas, join Shoes to Front and Back.
9. Referring to the photo for yarn colors, use overcast stitches to join unshaded edges of Front and Back.
10. Apply blush to Santa's face.

Finishing Options:

1. To join Santa in a Line-up, refer to Joining the Line-up on pg. 26 to hinge Santa to other Santas.
2. To use Santa by himself on a project, work stitches in pink shaded areas to join Front to Back.

Buckle
(6 x 5 threads)

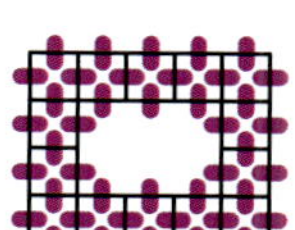

Belt (30 x 7 threads)

KEY

YARN	YARN
yellow	metallic gold
red	*black Fr. knot
sage	sage Turkey loop
lt brown	*Use 2 plies of yarn.
brown	

Bird #1
(6 x 5 threads)

Bird #2
(6 x 5 threads)
(stitch 2)

Tree (20 x 25 threads)

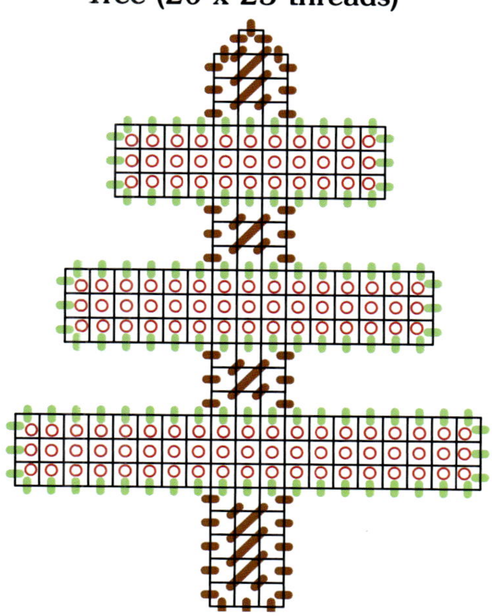

Shirt Trim
(3 x 26 threads)

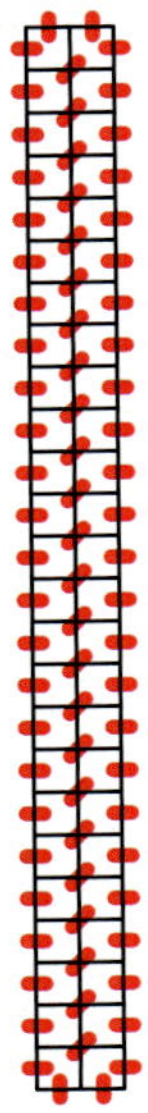

Mustache
(13 x 4 threads)

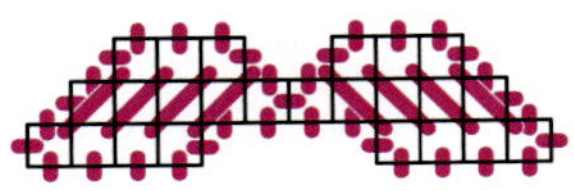

Hatchet Loop
(5 x 2 threads)

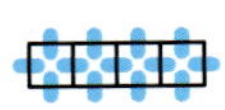

Hatchet
(6 x 14 threads)

KEY

YARN	YARN
white	brown
yellow	grey
flesh	black
red	
blue	**FLOSS (DMC)**
navy	*white (blanc)
dk green	*Use 6 strands of floss.

Nose
(4 x 4 threads) (cut 2)
Stack and stitch through two layers of canvas.

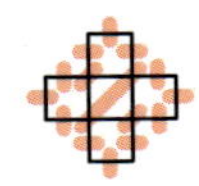

Beard (26 x 13 threads)
After working overcast stitches, refer to Diagram and tie 5" lengths of 6 strand white embroidery floss to threads to cover Beard. Trim ends.

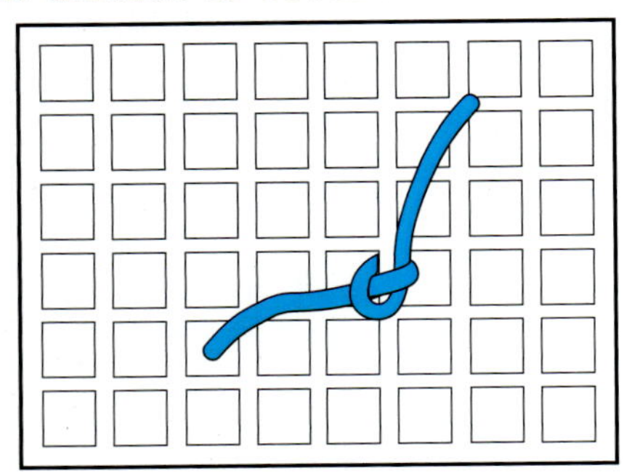

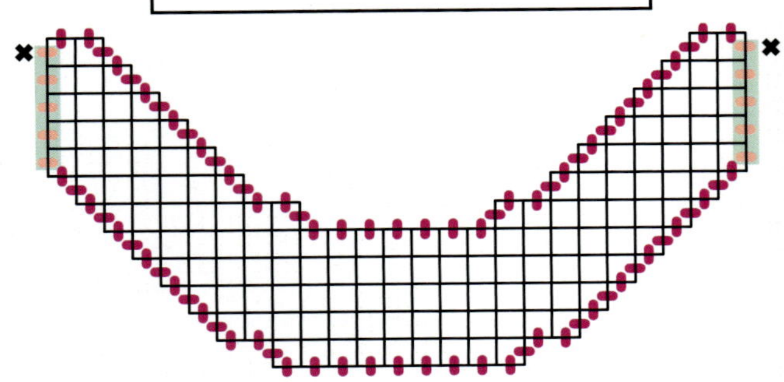

Front/Back
(30 x 84 threads) (cut 2) (stitch 1)

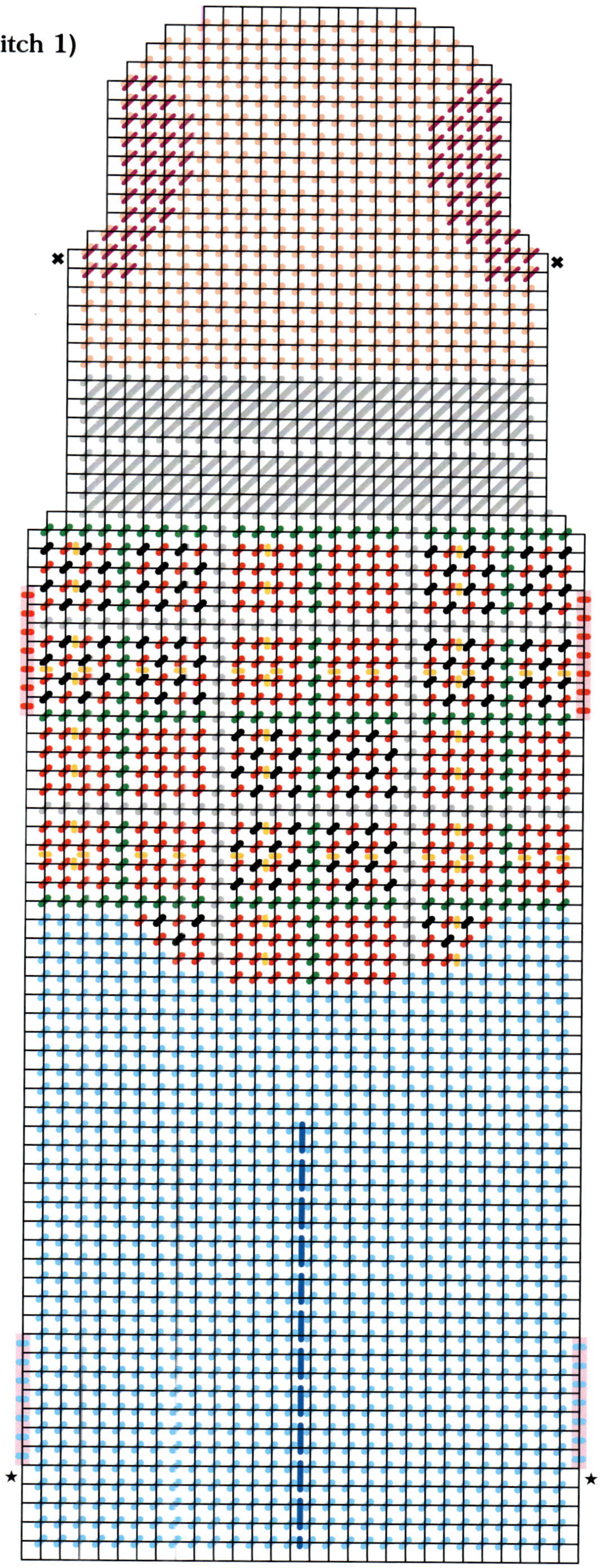

Belt Loop
(6 x 2 threads) (stitch 2)

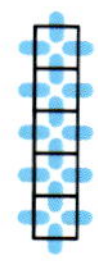

Eyebrow
(4 x 4 threads) (stitch 2)

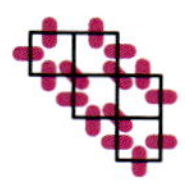

Cuffs
(30 x 11 threads)

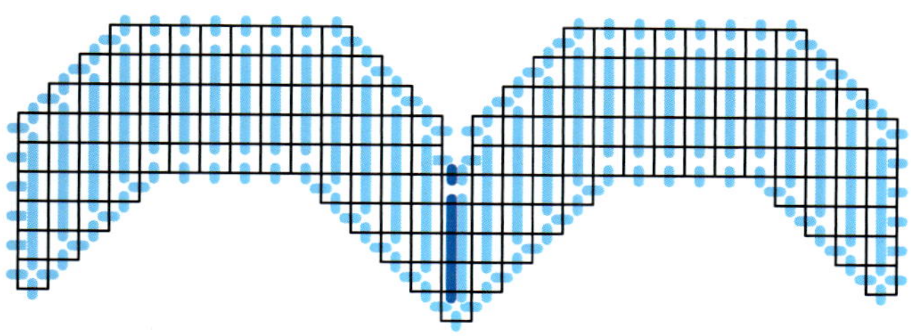

Arms
(30 x 20 threads)

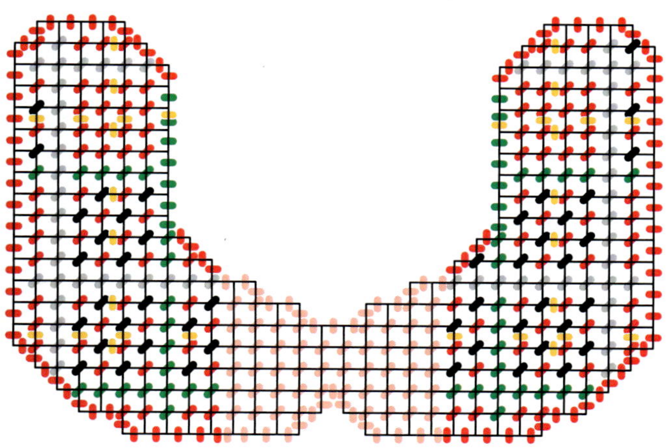

Shoes
(30 x 10 threads)

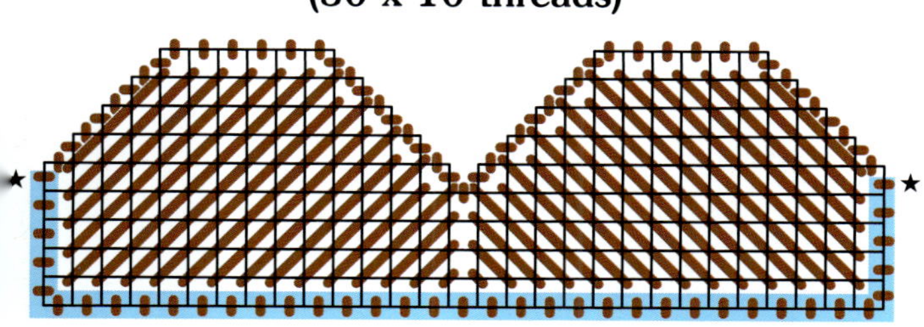

OLD WORLD SANTA

Size: $4^1/_2$"w x $12^3/_4$"h

Supplies: Worsted weight yarn, ecru Bernat Sparkle Christmas Yarn, and Rainbow Gallery metallic yarn for 7 mesh (refer to color key); two $10^1/_2$" x $13^1/_2$" sheets of clear 7 mesh plastic canvas; #16 tapestry needle; one 3" x 9" white foam board rectangle; two 12mm moveable eyes; 3" length of Needloft® metallic gold cord; paper clip; powder blush; and craft glue.

Instructions:

You will need to refer to the photo when assembling your Santa.

1. Follow charts to cut and stitch Santa pieces, leaving shaded areas unworked.

2. Tack Eyebrows, Nose, top edge of Mustache, and Beard to Front. Glue eyes to Front.

3. For Ornament, glue paper clip to wrong side of Ornament to form a hanger. Insert metallic gold cord through hanger on Ornament. Loop cord around Arms and secure ends to wrong side of Arms. Tack Arms to Front.

4. Placing foam board rectangle between Front and Back, use matching color overcast stitches to join unshaded edges of Front to Back.

5. Apply blush to Santa's face.

Finishing Options:

1. To join Santa in a Line-up, refer to Joining the Line-up on pg. 26 to hinge Santa to other Santas.

2. To use Santa by himself on a project, work stitches in pink shaded areas to join Front to Back.

KEY

YARN

- ecru sparkle
- flesh
- lt sage
- dk green
- metallic gold
- metallic red
- metallic silver

Eyebrow
(4 x 4 threads) (stitch 2)

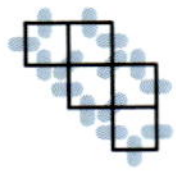

Nose
(4 x 4 threads) (cut 2)
Stack and stitch through two layers of canvas.

Arms
(30 x 20 threads)

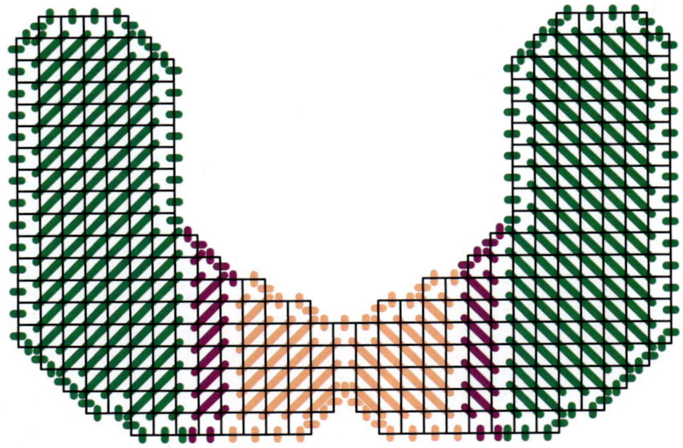

Mustache
(13 x 4 threads)

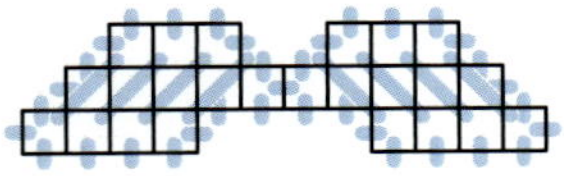

Front/Back
(30 x 84 threads) (cut 2) (stitch 1)

Ornament
(8 x 9 threads)

Beard (18 x 11 threads)
After working overcast stitches, refer to Diagram and
tie 14" lengths of ecru Bernat Sparkle Christmas Yarn
to threads to cover Beard.
Trim ends.

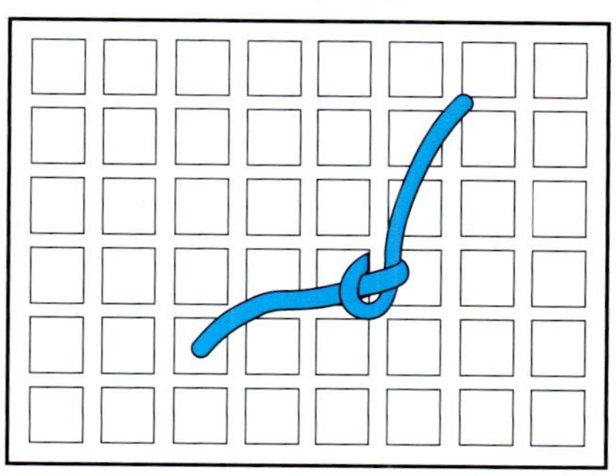

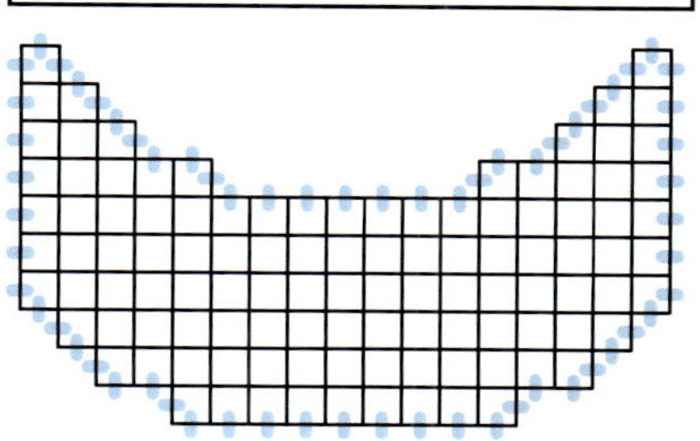

YULETIDE SANTA

Size: 4 1/2"w x 13 1/2"h
Supplies: Worsted weight yarn (refer to color key), two 10 1/2" x 13 1/2" sheets of clear 7 mesh plastic canvas, #16 tapestry needle, one 3" x 10" white foam board rectangle, two 12mm moveable eyes, powder blush, and craft glue.
Instructions:
You will need to refer to the photo when assembling your Santa.
1. Follow charts to cut and stitch Santa pieces, working backstitches and French knots last and leaving shaded areas unworked.
2. Tack Nose, top edge of Mustache, and Heart to Front. Glue eyes to Front.
3. Tack Candy Cane to Arms; tack Arms to Front.
4. Tack Bear to wrong side of Pocket; tack Paws to front of Pocket. Tack Pocket to Front.
5. Matching ★'s, tack bottom edge of Hat to Front. Working stitches in yellow shaded area and stitching through three layers of canvas, join Hat to Front and Back. Glue Eyebrows to Hat and Front.
6. Matching ✖'s, work stitches in green shaded areas through three layers of canvas to join Beard to Front and Back.
7. Placing foam board rectangle between Front and Back, use matching color overcast stitches to join unshaded edges of Front to Back.
8. Apply blush to Santa's face.

Finishing Options:
1. To join Santa in a Line-up, refer to Joining the Line-up on pg. 26 to hinge Santa to other Santas.
2. To use Santa by himself on a project, work stitches in pink shaded areas to join Front to Back.

KEY

YARN
- white
- flesh
- red
- lt blue
- dk blue
- lt brown
- grey
- black
- black Fr. knot

Eyebrow
(4 x 4 threads) (stitch 2)

Bear
(11 x 14 threads)

Paw
(5 x 5 threads)
(stitch 2)

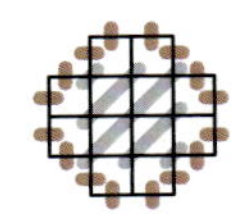

Hat
(27 x 19 threads)

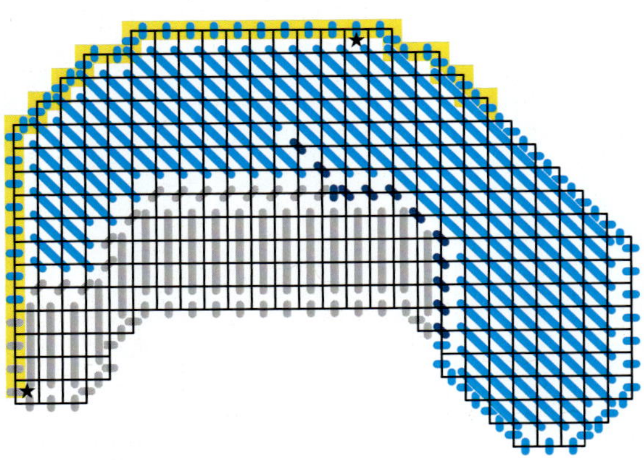

Arms
(30 x 20 threads)

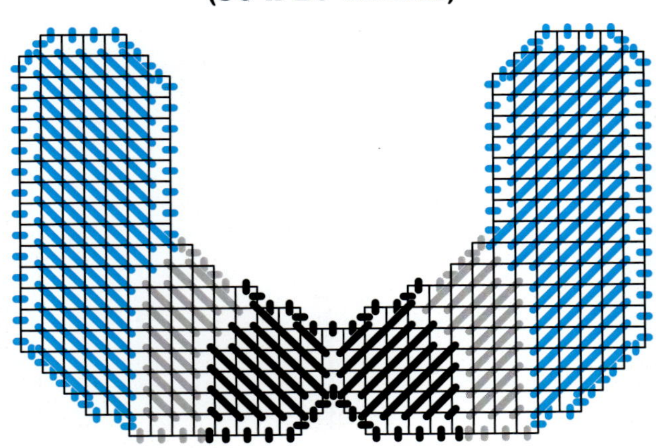

Front/Back
(30 x 89 threads) (cut 2) (stitch 1)

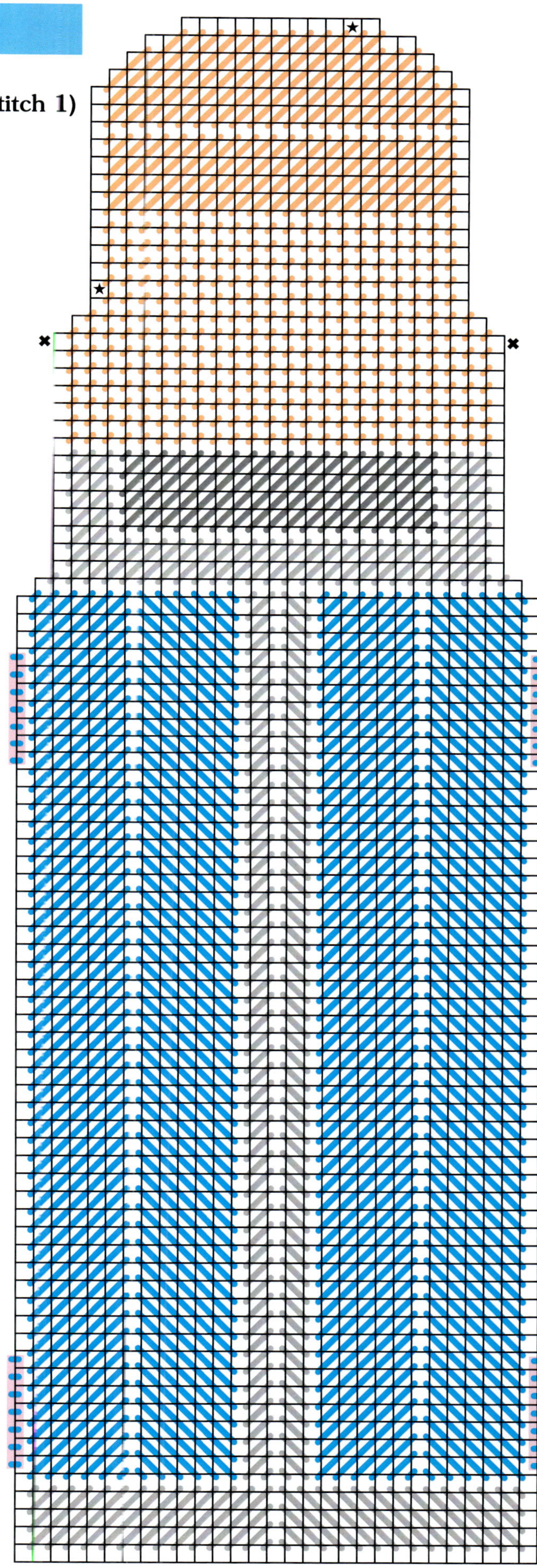

Heart
(8 x 8 threads)

Mustache
(13 x 4 threads)

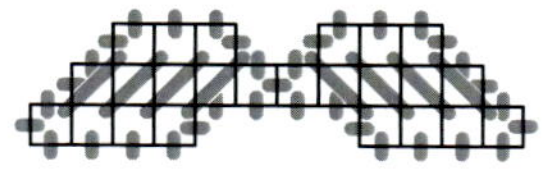

Nose
(4 x 4 threads) (cut 2)
Stack and stitch through two layers of canvas.

Pocket
(11 x 13 threads)

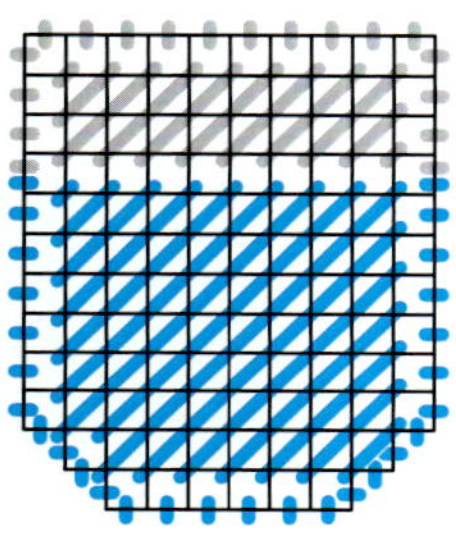

Candy Cane
(11 x 20 threads)

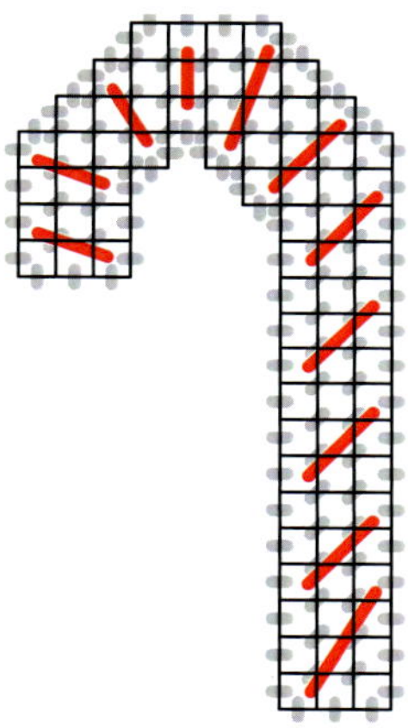

Beard (26 x 13 threads)
After working overcast stitches, refer to Diagram and tie 4" lengths of grey yarn to threads to cover Beard. Trim ends.

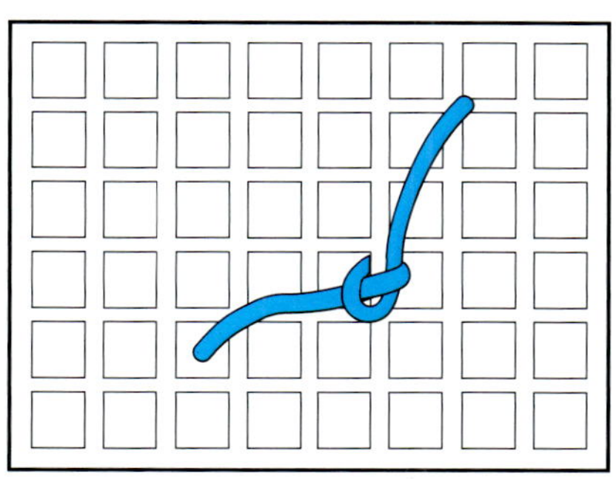

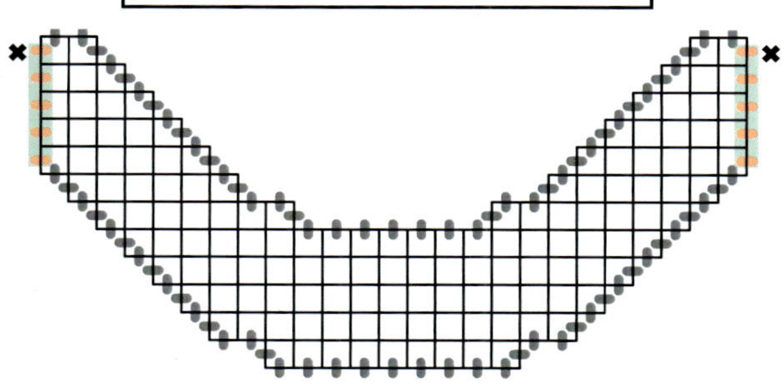

HOLLY JOLLY SANTA

Size: 4$^1/_2$"w x 13$^1/_4$"h
Supplies: Worsted weight yarn (refer to color key), two 10$^1/_2$" x 13$^1/_2$" sheets of clear 7 mesh plastic canvas, #16 tapestry needle, one 3" x 10" white foam board rectangle, two 12mm moveable eyes, 3" x 2" cardboard rectangle, powder blush, and craft glue.
Instructions:
You will need to refer to the photo when assembling your Santa.
1. Follow charts to cut and stitch Santa pieces, working French knots last and leaving shaded areas unworked.
2. Tack Nose and top edge of Mustache to Front. Glue eyes to Front.
3. Insert Arms through Wreath. Tack Arms and Wreath to Front.
4. Matching ★'s, tack bottom edge of Hat to Front. Working stitches in yellow shaded area and stitching through three layers of canvas, join Hat to Front and Back. Glue Eyebrows to Hat and Front.
5. Matching ✖'s, work stitches in green shaded areas through three layers of canvas to join Beard to Front and Back.
6. Matching ♥'s, tack top of Shoes to Front. Place foam board rectangle between Front and Back. Working stitches in blue shaded area and stitching through three layers of canvas, join Shoes to Front and Back.
7. Referring to photo for yarn colors, use overcast stitches to join unshaded edges of Front and Back.
8. To make pom-pom for Hat, cut a 5" length of ecru yarn. Referring to Diagram A on pg. 28, wrap three yards of ecru yarn around cardboard. Remove cardboard from yarn circle. Referring to Diagram B on pg. 28, tie 5" length of yarn around center of yarn circle. Clip loops of yarn circle. Trim ends to shape. Glue pom-pom to Hat.
8. Apply blush to Santa's face.

Finishing Options:
1. To join Santa in a Line-up, refer to Joining the Line-up on pg. 26 to hinge Santa to other Santas.
2. To use Santa by himself on a project, work stitches in pink shaded areas to join Front to Back.

KEY

YARN	YARN
ecru	green
flesh	black
dk red	red Fr. knot

Eyebrow
(4 x 4 threads) (stitch 2)

Beard (26 x 13 threads)
After working overcast stitches, refer to Diagram and tie 4" lengths of ecru yarn to threads to cover Beard. Trim ends.

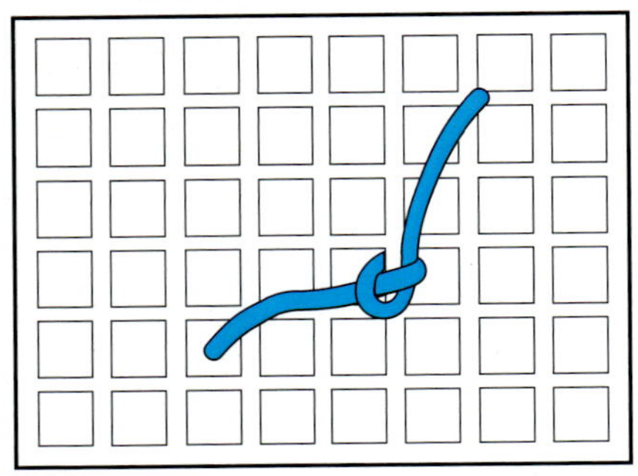

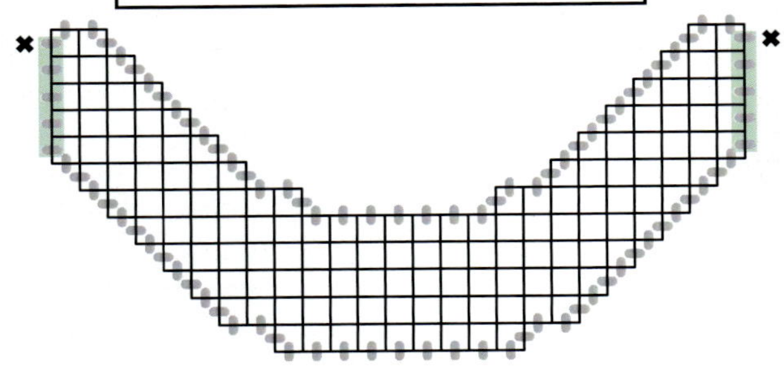

Arms
(30 x 20 threads)

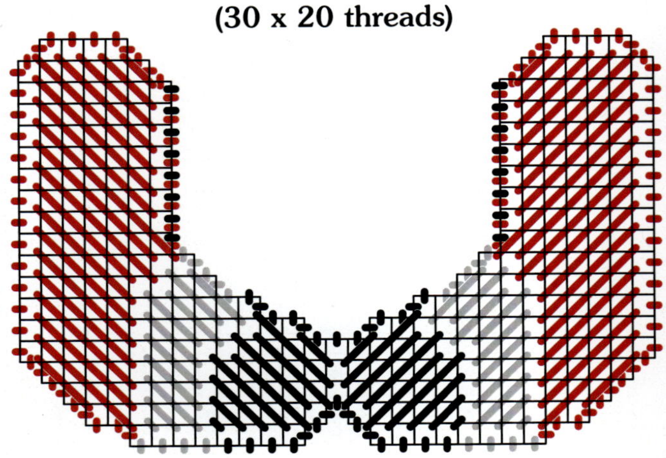

Shoes
(30 x 10 threads)

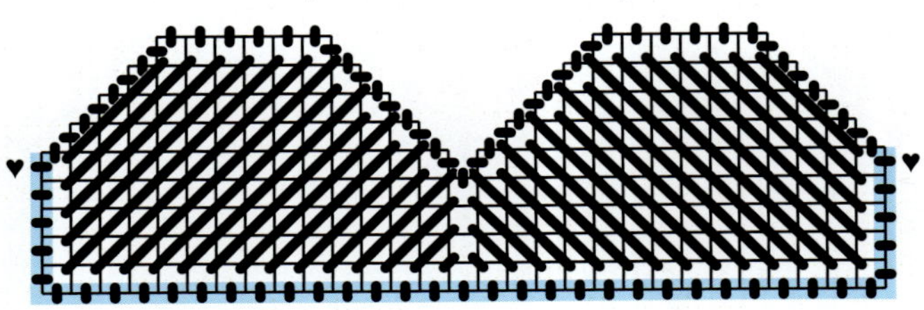

Front/Back
(30 x 88 threads) (cut 2) (stitch 1)

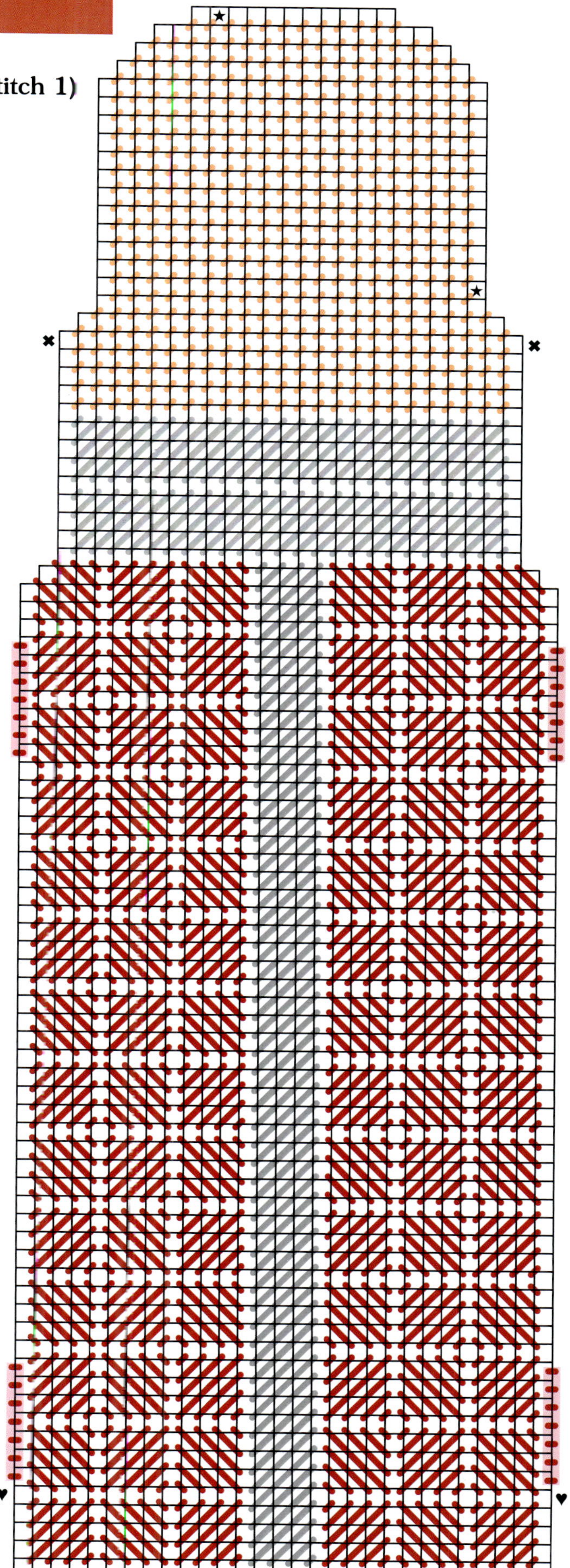

Nose
(4 x 4 threads) (cut 2)
Stack and stitch through two layers of canvas.

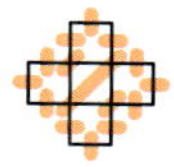

Mustache
(13 x 4 threads)

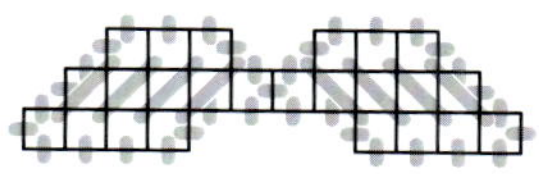

Hat
(27 x 19 threads)

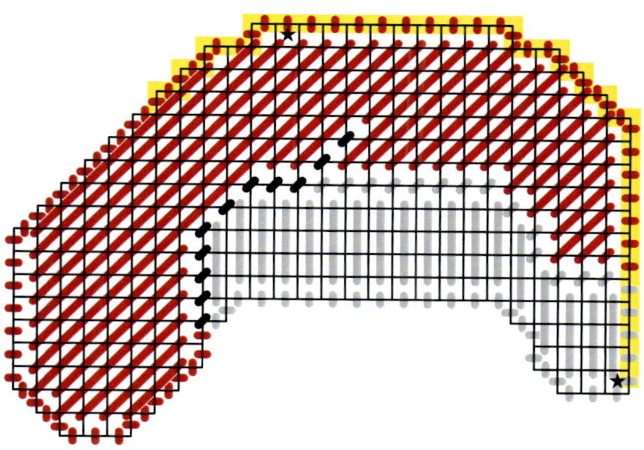

Wreath
(24 x 24 threads)

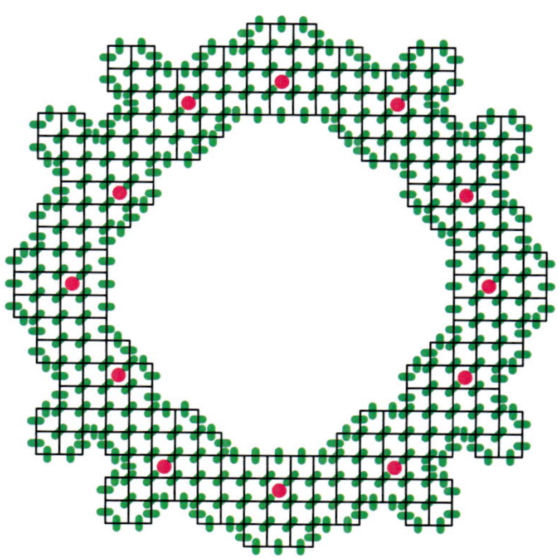

Special Project!

GIFT BOX

Make any gift special with this jolly Old St. Nick Gift Box. It's just the right size for a bottle of bubbly.

Gift Box Size: 5"w x 13 3/4"h x 5"d, excluding ribbon

Supplies for Gift Box: Green worsted weight yarn, three 10 1/2" x 13 1/2" sheets of clear 7 mesh plastic canvas, #16 tapestry needle, and desired ribbons and bow.

Instructions:

To stitch and assemble your Gift Box:

1. For Top Sides, cut four 34 x 10 thread pieces of plastic canvas. For Top, cut one 34 x 34 thread piece of plastic canvas. For Bottom Sides, cut four 32 x 90 thread pieces of plastic canvas. For Bottom, cut one 32 x 32 thread piece of plastic canvas.

2. Referring to photo for pattern, cover pieces with green Gobelin stitches over two threads.

3. Using green overcast stitches, join Top Sides along short edges. Join Top to Top Sides. Join Bottom Sides along long edges. Join Bottom to Bottom Sides. Cover unworked edges.

4. Add ribbons and bow as desired.

5. Follow the instructions on pg. 18 to stitch and assemble Old St. Nick. Tack Santa to Gift Box.

Special Project!

DOORSTOP

Hold the door open and welcome those holiday guests with this Old World Doorstop.

Doorstop Size: 4"w x 8 1/4"h x 2 1/2"d

Supplies for Doorstop: Dk green worsted weight yarn, two 10 1/2" x 13 1/2" sheets of clear 7 mesh plastic canvas, #16 tapestry needle, 3 1/2"w x 7 1/2"h x 2 1/8"d brick, and plastic wrap.

Instructions:

To stitch and assemble your Doorstop:

1. For Front and Back, cut two 27 x 57 thread pieces of plastic canvas. For Sides, cut two 17 x 57 thread pieces of plastic canvas. For Top and Bottom, cut two 27 x 17 thread pieces of plastic canvas.

2. Cover pieces with dk green Gobelin stitches over five threads.

3. Using dk green overcast stitches, join Front, Back, and Sides along long edges. Join Top to Front, Back, and Sides.

4. Follow the instructions on pg. 8 to stitch and assemble Old World Santa. Tack Santa to Front.

5. Wrap brick with plastic wrap. Insert brick in Doorstop. Join Bottom to Front, Back, and Sides.

Special Project!

WREATH

Create a festive door decoration. Just follow the instructions on pg. 24 to stitch and assemble Joyful Santa. Attach Santa to a wreath and add other embellishments as desired.

Special Project!

ALL-AMERICAN CENTERPIECE

For a patriotic touch, just follow the instructions on pg. 22 to stitch and assemble All-American Santa. Attach Santa to a 10"h x 6" dia. aluminum bucket and add a bouquet of American flags.

OLD ST. NICK

Size: 4 1/2"w x 14 3/4"h

Supplies: Worsted weight yarn and Rainbow Gallery metallic gold yarn for 7 mesh (refer to color key), two 10 1/2" x 13 1/2" sheets of clear 7 mesh plastic canvas, #16 tapestry needle, one 3" x 10" white foam board rectangle, two 12mm moveable eyes, powder blush, and craft glue.

Instructions:

You will need to refer to the photo when assembling your Santa.

1. Follow charts to cut and stitch Santa pieces, working backstitch, French knots, and Turkey loops last and leaving shaded areas unworked.

2. Tack Eyebrows, Nose, and top edge of Mustache to Front. Glue eyes to Front.

3. Tack Bear to wrong side of Arms; tack Paws to Bear and Arms. Tack Arms to Front.

4. Matching ♥'s, tack bottom edge of Hat to Santa Front. Working stitches in yellow shaded areas and stitching through three layers of canvas, join Hat to Front and Back.

5. Matching ✖'s, work stitches in green shaded areas through three layers of canvas to join Beard to Front and Back.

6. Tack Buckle to Belt. Matching ■'s, work stitches in lavender shaded areas through three layers of canvas to join Belt to Front and Back

7. Matching ★'s, tack top of Shoes to Front. Place foam board rectangle between Front and Back. Working stitches in blue shaded area and stitching through three layers of canvas, join Shoes to Front and Back.

8. Referring to photo for yarn colors, use overcast stitches to join unshaded edges of Front and Back.

9. Apply blush to Santa's face.

Finishing Options:

1. To join Santa in a Line-up, refer to Joining the Line-up on pg. 26 to hinge Santa to other Santas.

2. To use Santa by himself on a project, work stitches in pink shaded areas to join Front to Back.

Mustache (13 x 4 threads)

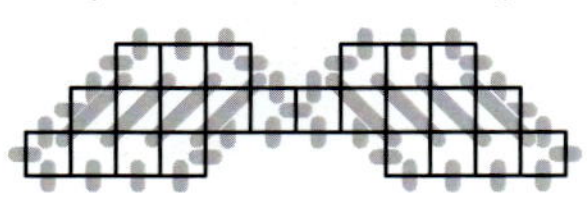

Beard (26 x 13 threads)

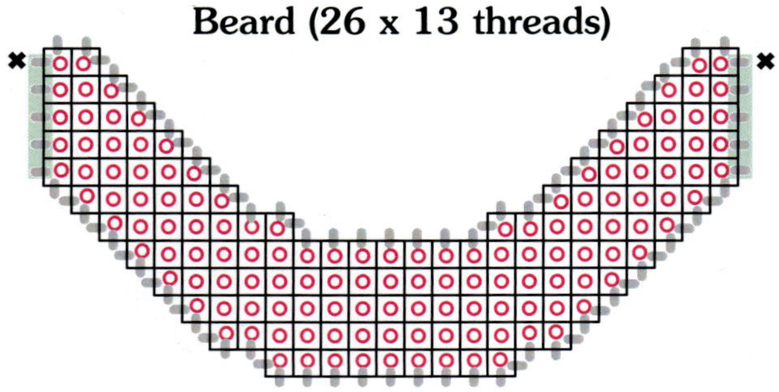

KEY

YARN	YARN
white	black
flesh	metallic gold
red	black Fr. knot
dk red	white Turkey loop
lt brown	

Belt (30 x 4 threads)

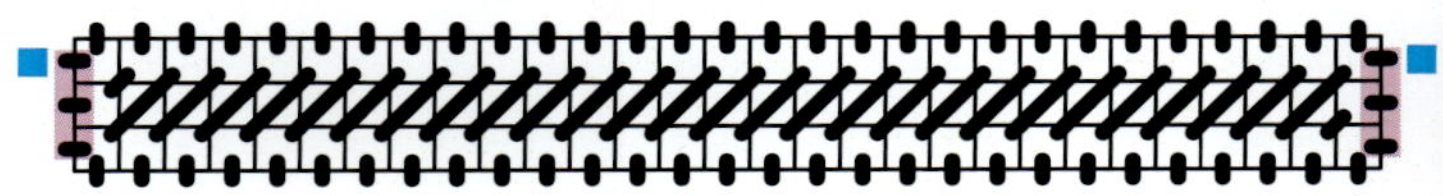

Hat
(22 x 26 threads)
After working stitches on chart, refer to Diagram and tie 2" lengths of white yarn to threads to cover pom-pom on Hat. Trim ends.

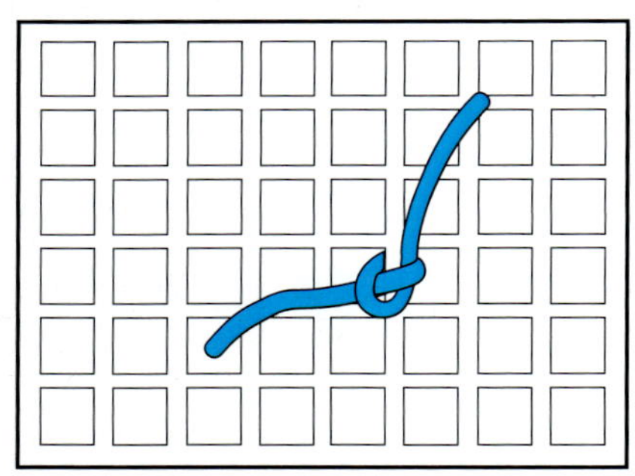

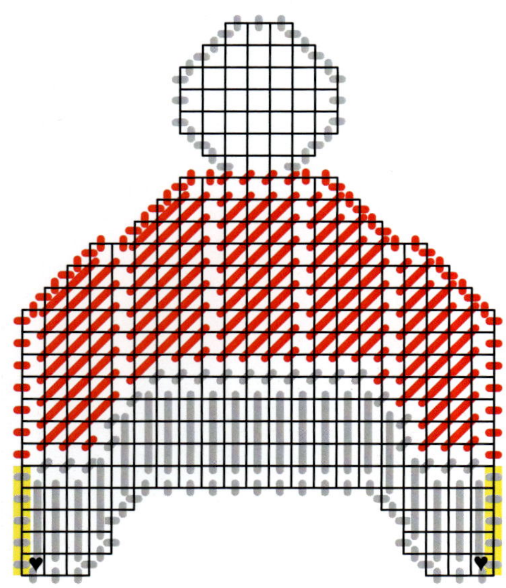

Buckle
(8 x 8 threads)

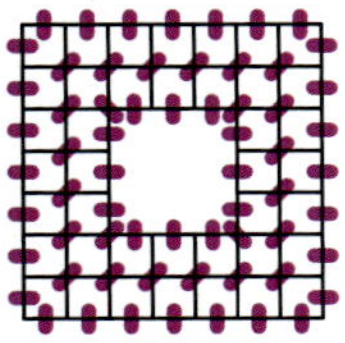

Front/Back
(30 x 85 threads) (cut 2) (stitch 1)

Eyebrow
(4 x 4 threads) (stitch 2)

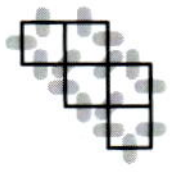

Nose
(4 x 4 threads) (cut 2)
Stack and stitch through two layers of canvas.

Paw
(5 x 5 threads)
(stitch 2)

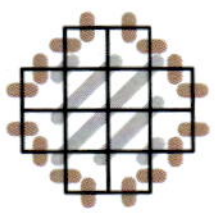

Bear
(11 x 14 threads)

Arms
(30 x 20 threads)

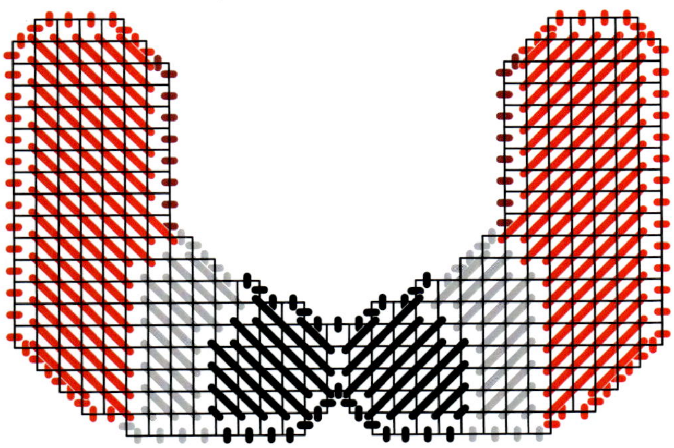

Shoes
(30 x 10 threads)

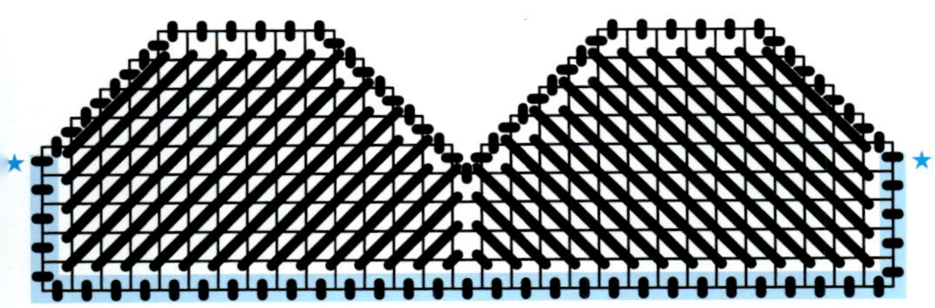

STARLIGHT SANTA

Size: 5"w x 14 3/4"h

Supplies: Worsted weight yarn and beige postal string (refer to color key), two 10 1/2" x 13 1/2" sheets of clear 7 mesh plastic canvas, #16 tapestry needle, one 3" x 10" white foam board rectangle, two 12mm moveable eyes, two 6" lengths of Needloft® metallic gold cord, powder blush, and craft glue.

Instructions:

You will need to refer to the photo when assembling your Santa.

1. Follow charts to cut and stitch Santa pieces, working Turkey loops last and leaving shaded areas unworked.
2. Tack Nose, top edge of Mustache, and Arms to Front. Glue eyes to Front.
3. Matching ★'s, tack bottom edge of Hat to Front. Working stitches in yellow shaded areas and stitching through three layers of canvas, join Hat to Front and Back. Glue Eyebrows to Hat and Front.
4. Matching ✖'s, work stitches in green shaded areas through three layers of canvas to join Beard to Front and Back.
5. Placing foam board rectangle between Front and Back, use matching color overcast stitches to join unshaded edges of Front to Back.
6. Secure one Star on each end of one length of cord. Loop cord over Arms and secure cord to wrong side of Arms. Secure one Star on each end and in the center of second length of gold cord. Tack center Star to Arms.
7. Apply blush to Santa's face.

Finishing Options:

1. To join Santa in a Line-up, refer to Joining the Line-up on pg. 26 to hinge Santa to other Santas.
2. To use Santa by himself on a project, work stitches in pink shaded areas to join Front to Back.

Mustache
(13 x 4 threads)

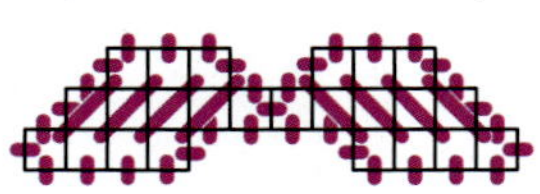

KEY

YARN

- yellow
- flesh
- lt sage
- grey
- black
- *beige
- grey Turkey loop

*Use beige postal string.

Nose
(4 x 4 threads) (cut 2)
Stack and stitch through two layers of canvas.

Eyebrow
(4 x 4 threads) (stitch 2)

Beard (26 x 13 threads)
After working overcast stitches, refer to Diagram and tie 7" lengths of beige postal string to threads to cover Beard. Trim ends.

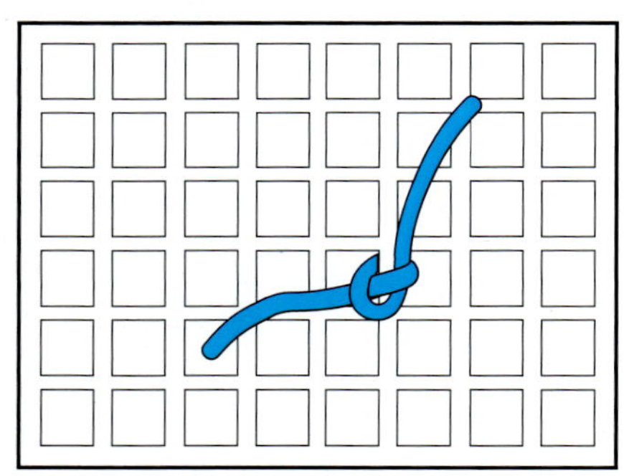

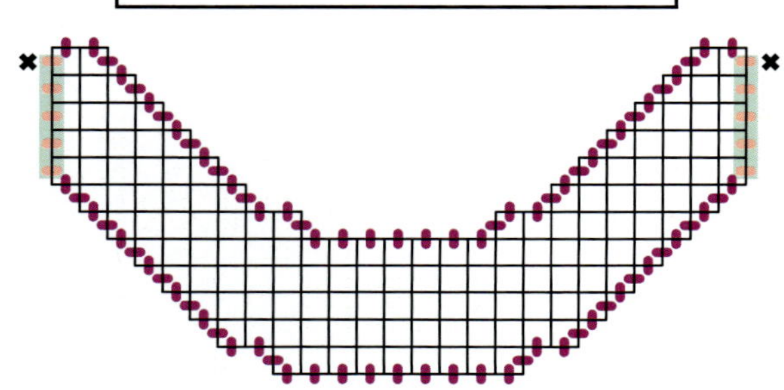

Front/Back
(30 x 89 threads) (cut 2) (stitch 1)

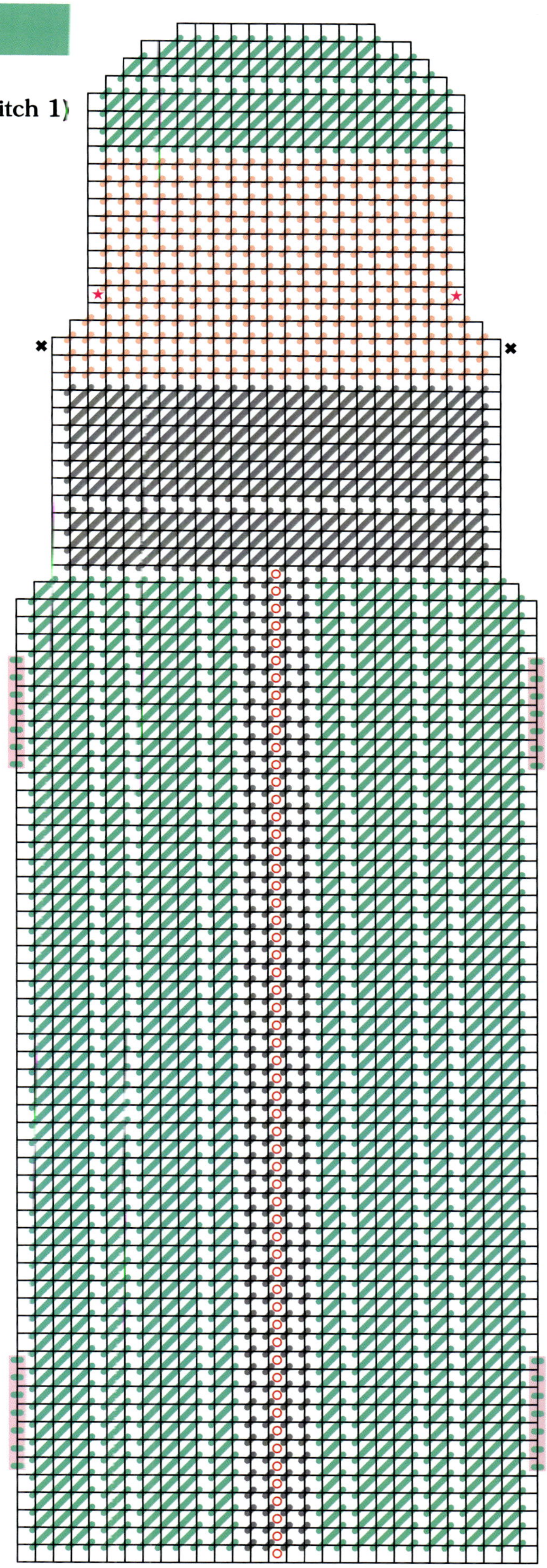

Star
(10 x 10 threads) (stitch 5)

Hat
(22 x 26 threads)

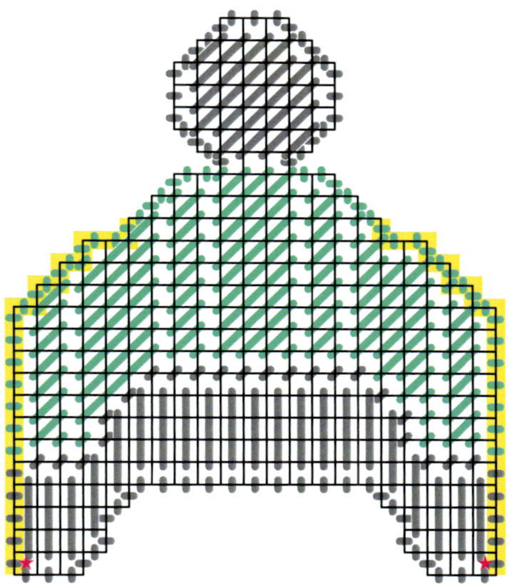

Arms
(30 x 20 threads)

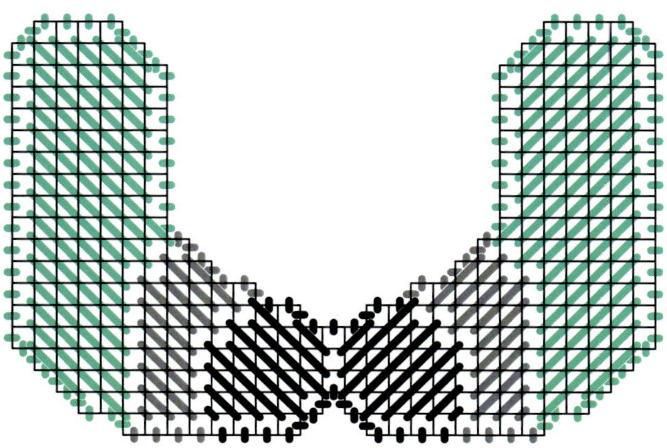

ALL-AMERICAN SANTA

Size: 4 1/2"w x 14 1/2"h
Supplies: Worsted weight yarn, white sport weight yarn, and Rainbow Gallery metallic gold yarn for 7 mesh (refer to color key); two 10 1/2" x 13 1/2" sheets of clear 7 mesh plastic canvas; #16 tapestry needle; one 3" x 10" white foam board rectangle; two 12mm moveable eyes; four gold buttons; 3" x 2" cardboard rectangle; powder blush; and craft glue.
Instructions:
You will need to refer to the photo when assembling your Santa.
1. Follow charts to cut and stitch Santa pieces, working backstitches and French knots last and leaving shaded areas unworked.
2. Tack Eyebrows, Nose, top edge of Mustache, and Arms to Front. Glue eyes and buttons to Front.
3. Tack Watch to wrong side of Pocket. Tack Pockets to Front.
4. Matching ♥'s, tack bottom edge of Hat to Front. Working stitches in yellow shaded area and stitching through three layers of canvas, join Hat to Front and Back.
5. Matching ■'s, work stitches in green shaded areas through three layers of canvas to join Beard to Front and Back.
6. Matching ★'s, tack top of Shoes to Front. Place foam board rectangle between Front and Back. Working stitches in blue shaded area and stitching through three layers of canvas, join Shoes to Front and Back.
7. Using matching color overcast stitches, join unshaded edges of Front and Back.
8. To make pom-pom for Hat, cut a 5" length of white yarn. Referring to Diagram A on pg. 28, wrap one yard each of red, white, and navy yarn around cardboard. Remove cardboard from yarn circle. Referring to Diagram B on pg. 28, tie 5" length of yarn around center of yarn circle. Clip loops of yarn circle. Trim ends to shape. Glue pom-pom to Hat.
8. Apply blush to Santa's face.

Finishing Options:
1. To join Santa in a Line-up, refer to Joining the Line-up on pg. 26 to hinge Santa to other Santas.
2. To use Santa by himself on a project, work stitches in pink shaded areas to join Front to Back.

KEY

YARN	YARN
white	black
flesh	metallic gold
red	*black Fr. knot
dk red	*Use 2 plies of yarn.
navy	

Nose
(4 x 4 threads) (cut 2)
Stack and stitch through two layers of canvas.

Beard (26 x 13 threads)
After working overcast stitches, refer to Diagram and tie 5" lengths of white sport weight yarn to threads to cover Beard. Trim ends.

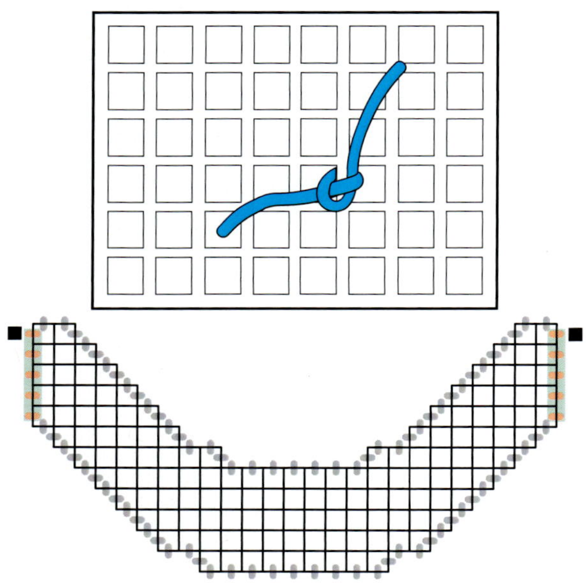

Mustache
(13 x 4 threads)

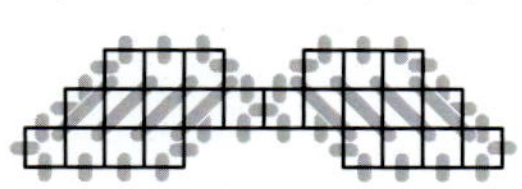

Pocket
(8 x 6 threads) (stitch 2)

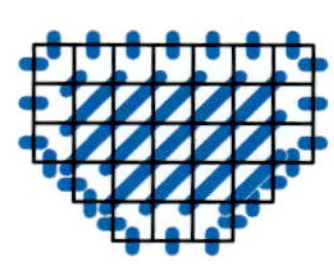

Watch
(8 x 10 threads)

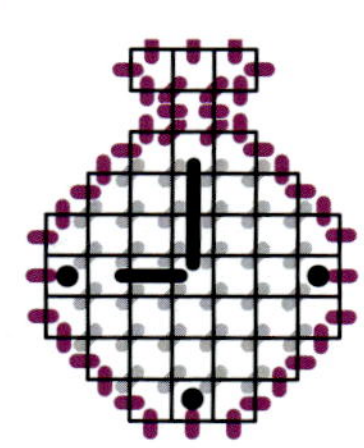

Front/Back
(30 x 91 threads) (cut 2) (stitch 1)

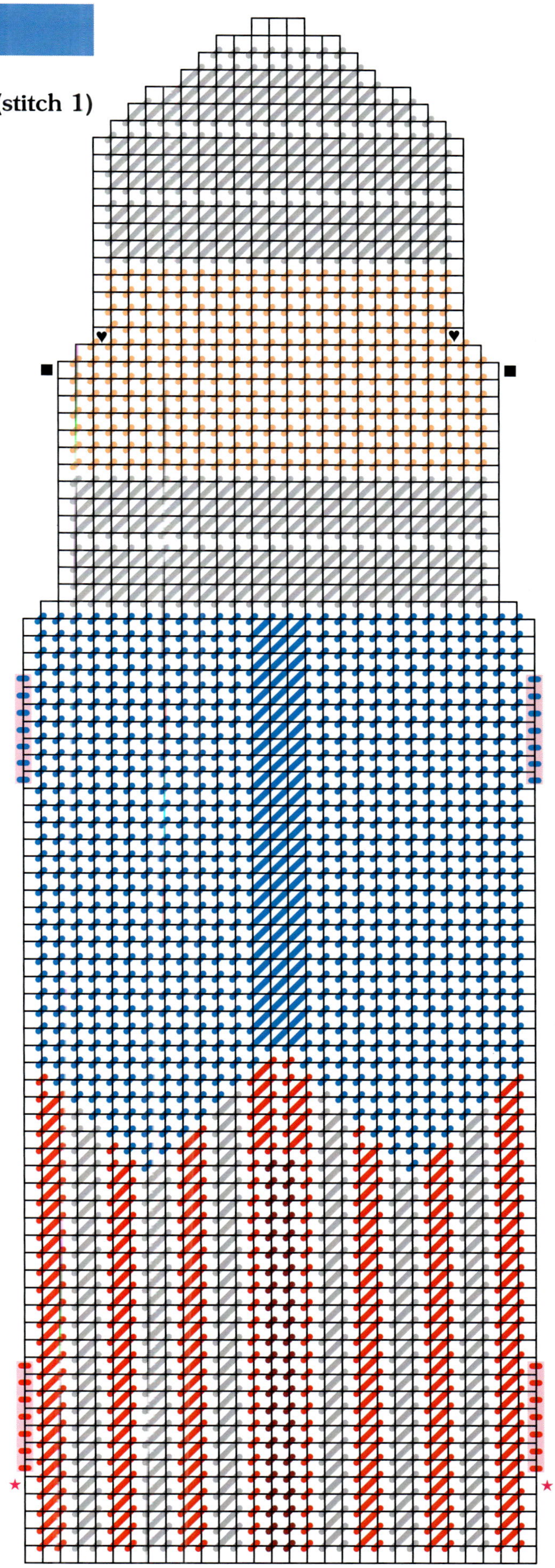

Eyebrow
(4 x 4 threads) (stitch 2)

Hat
(22 x 26 threads)

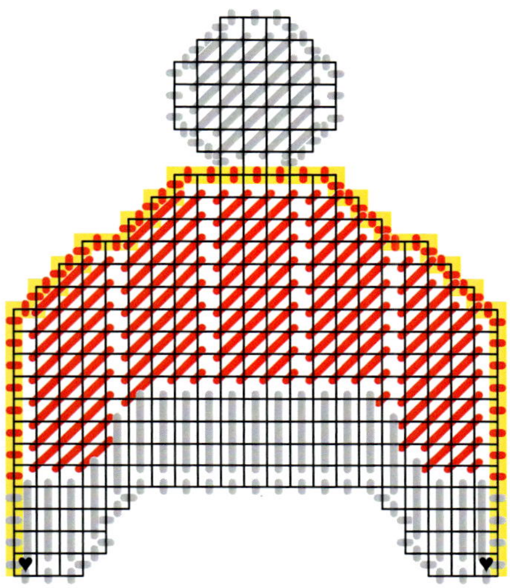

Arms
(30 x 20 threads)

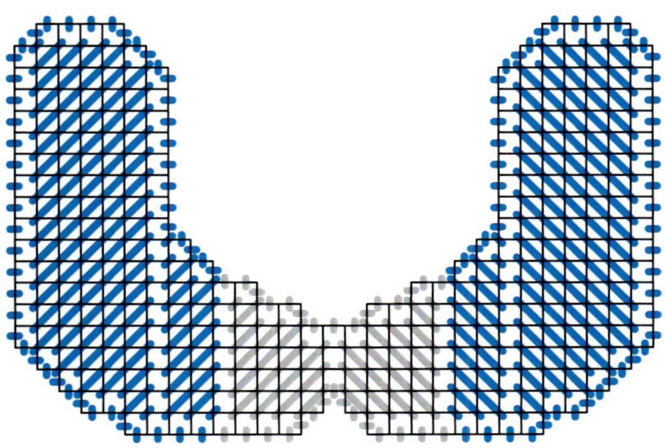

Shoes
(30 x 10 threads)

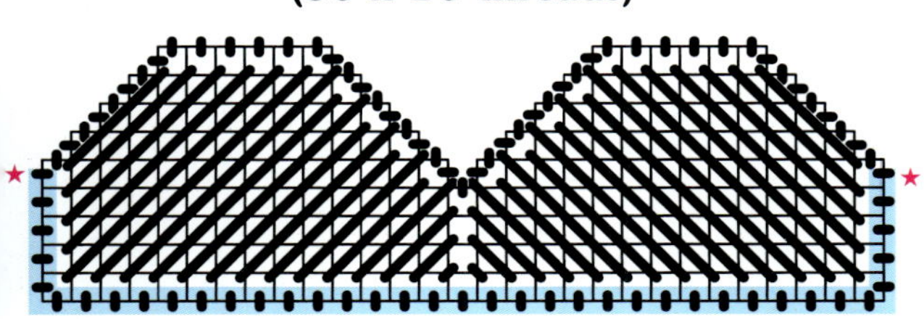

JOYFUL SANTA

Size: 4 1/2"w x 13"h
Supplies: Worsted weight yarn and Rainbow Gallery metallic gold yarn for 7 mesh (refer to color key), two 10 1/2" x 13 1/2" sheets of clear 7 mesh plastic canvas, #16 tapestry needle, one 3" x 10" white foam board rectangle, two 12mm moveable eyes, 36" length of 1/8"w red ribbon, powder blush, and craft glue.
Instructions:
You will need to refer to the photo when assembling your Santa.
1. Follow charts to cut and stitch Santa pieces, working backstitches, French knots, and Turkey loops last and leaving shaded areas unworked.
2. Tack Eyebrows, Nose, top edge of Mustache, Hat Band, Trim A, and Trim B to Front. Glue eyes to Front.
3. Tack Arms to Front.
4. Matching ★'s, work stitches in green shaded areas through three layers of canvas to join Beard to Front and Back.
5. Placing foam board rectangle between Front and Back, use matching color overcast stitches to join unshaded edges of Front to Back.
6. Tie ribbon around Horn. Loop ribbon around Arms. Tie bow and trim ends.
7. Apply blush to Santa's face.

Finishing Options:
1. To join Santa in a Line-up, refer to Joining the Line-up on pg. 26 to hinge Santa to other Santas.
2. To use Santa by himself on a project, work stitches in pink shaded areas to join Front to Back.

KEY

YARN
- ecru
- lt gold
- gold
- flesh
- lt pink
- metallic gold
- metallic gold Fr. knot
- ecru Turkey loop

Nose
(4 x 4 threads) (cut 2)
Stack and stitch through two layers of canvas.

Arms
(30 x 20 threads)

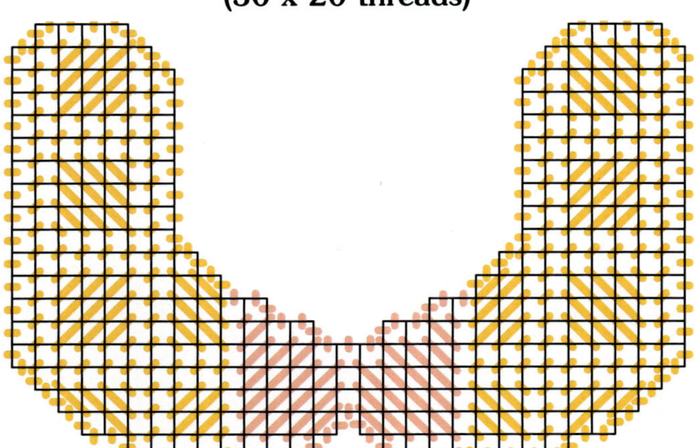

Trim A
(14 x 56 threads)

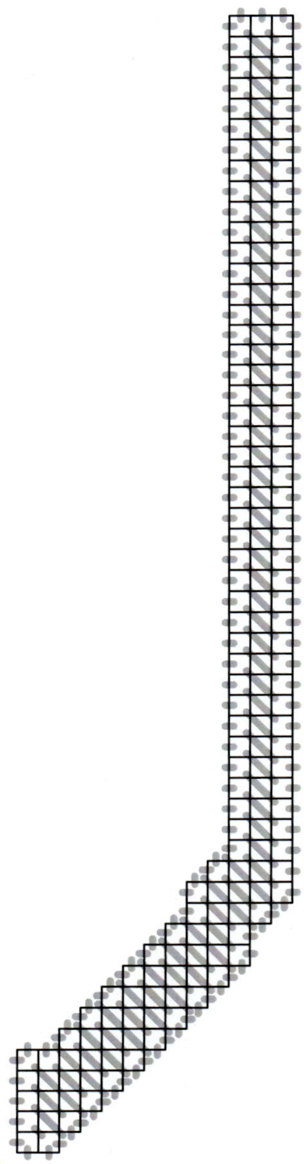

Trim B
(14 x 56 threads)

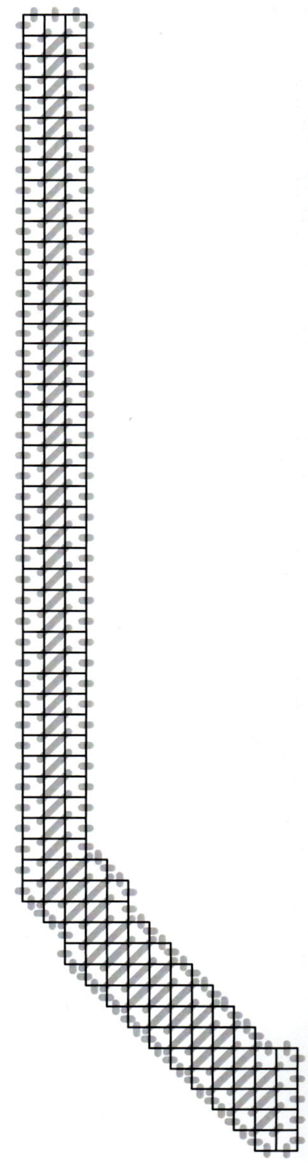

Front/Back
(30 x 86 threads) (cut 2) (stitch 1)

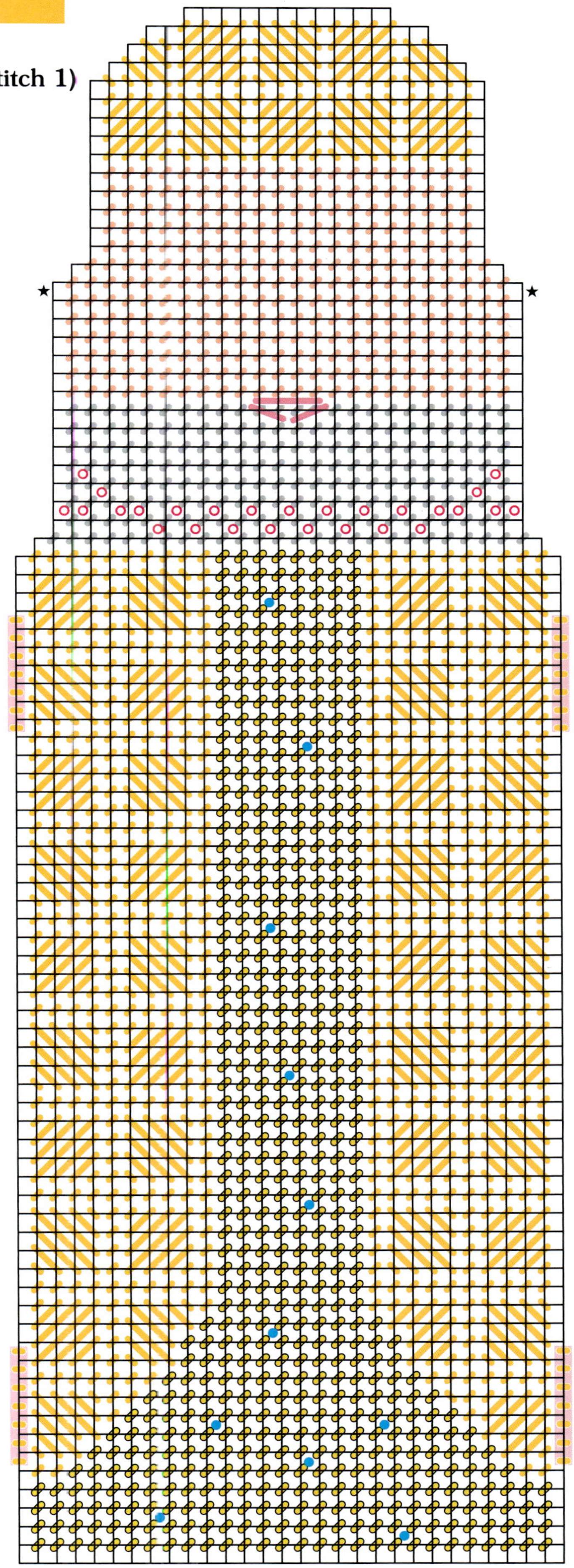

Mustache
(13 x 4 threads)

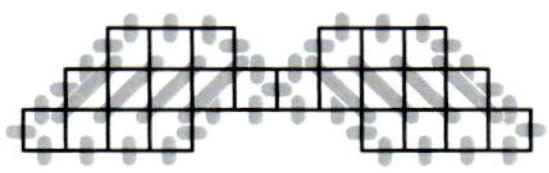

Eyebrow
(4 x 4 threads) (stitch 2)

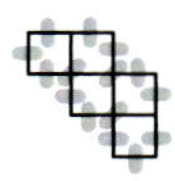

Hat Band
(26 x 11 threads)

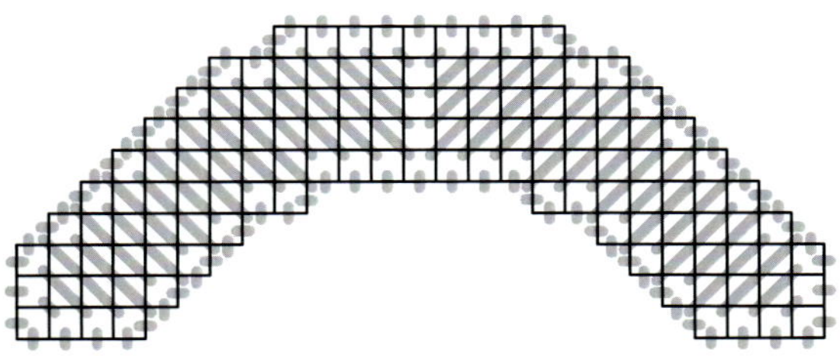

Horn
(15 x 9 threads)

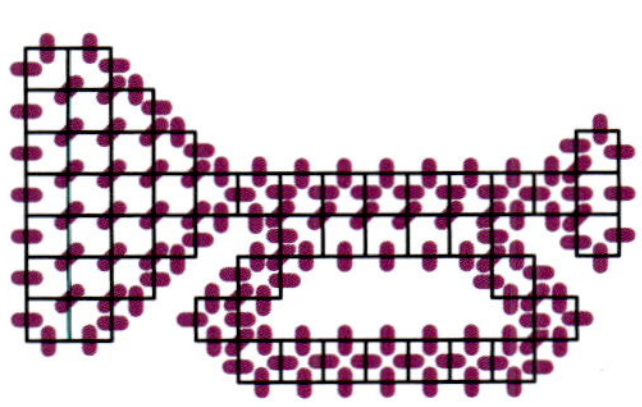

Beard (26 x 13 threads)

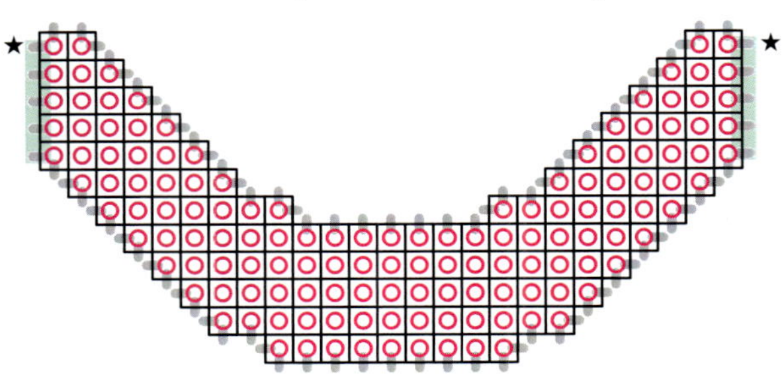

JOINING THE LINE-UP

Join the Santas in any combination to create festive holiday decorations. Just follow the instructions included below to hinge your Santas together.

Instructions:

1. Follow the instructions on the chart pages to assemble your favorite Santas.

2. Following the Hinge chart below, cut and stitch the necessary number of Hinges using Rainbow Gallery metallic gold yarn for 7 mesh canvas.

Hinge (14 x 7 threads)
Cut from clear 7 mesh plastic canvas.

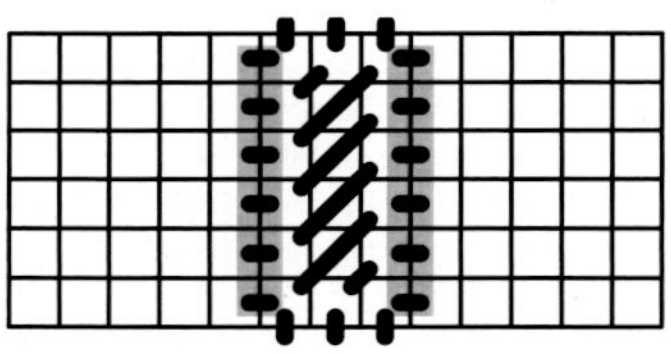

3. Work stitches in pink shaded areas on each Santa to cover unworked edges of Front only.

4. Insert Hinges in openings between Front and Back on each Santa. Work stitches in grey shaded areas on each Hinge to join Hinges to unworked edges of Back only.

PLASTIC CANVAS BASICS

WORKING WITH PLASTIC CANVAS

Counting Threads. Throughout this leaflet, the lines of the canvas will be referred to as threads. However, they are not actually "threads" since the canvas is not woven. Before cutting out your pieces, note the thread count of each chart. The thread count is listed above the chart and indicates the number of threads in the width and height of the canvas pieces. To cut plastic canvas pieces accurately, count **threads** (not **holes**) as shown in **Fig. 1**.

Fig. 1

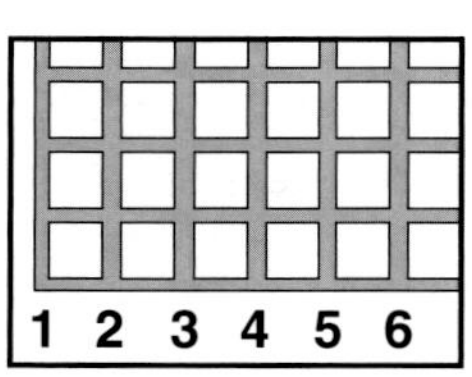

Marking the Canvas. If you find it necessary to mark on the canvas, use an overhead projector pen. Outline shape with pen, cut out shape, and remove markings with water and a towel.

Cutting the Canvas. When cutting canvas, make sure to cut as close to the thread as possible without cutting into the thread. If you don't cut close enough, "nubs" or "pickets" will be left on the edge of your canvas. Make sure to cut off all nubs from the canvas before you begin to stitch because nubs will snag the yarn or floss and are difficult to cover. A craft knife is helpful when cutting a small area from the center of a larger piece of canvas. When using a craft knife, protect the table below your canvas with a layer of cardboard or a magazine.

WORKING WITH YARN AND FLOSS

Selecting Yarn or Floss. We used various brands of worsted weight yarn, sport weight yarn, metallic yarn, and embroidery floss to stitch the photography models for this leaflet. If you can't find sport weight yarn in the color needed, worsted weight yarn may be substituted; simply remove one ply of the yarn and stitch with the remaining three plies.

Separating Yarn Strands. Most brands of worsted weight yarn have four plies that are twisted together to form one strand. When the instructions say to use two plies of yarn, simply remove two plies of the worsted weight yarn and stitch with the remaining two plies.

Separating Floss Strands. DMC Embroidery Floss was used for the projects in this leaflet. Embroidery floss is made up of six strands that are twisted together. To ensure smoother stitches, separate strands and realign them before threading needle.

Dye Lot Variations. It is important to buy all of the yarn or floss you need to complete your project from the same dye lot. Although variations in color may be slight when yarns or flosses from two different dye lots are held together, the variation is usually apparent on a stitched piece.

READING THE COLOR KEY

Color keys are included for each project. The key indicates the types and colors of yarn or floss used and how each color is represented on the chart. For example, when white yarn is represented by a grey line in the color key, all grey stitches on the chart should be stitched using white yarn.

READING THE CHART

Whenever possible, the drawing on the chart looks like the completed stitch. For example, the tent stitches on the chart are drawn diagonally across one intersection of threads just like tent stitches look on your piece of canvas. Likewise, Gobelin stitches on the chart look identical to the Gobelin stitches on your canvas. When a stitch cannot clearly be drawn on the chart, like a French knot, a symbol will be used instead. If you have difficulty determining how a particular stitch is worked, refer to Stitch Diagrams.

STITCHING THE DESIGN

Securing the First Stitch. Don't knot the end of your yarn or floss before you begin stitching. Instead, begin each length of yarn or floss by coming up from the wrong side of the canvas and leaving a 1" - 2" tail on the wrong side. Hold this tail against the canvas and work the first few stitches over the tail. When secure, clip the tail close to your stitched piece. Clipping the tail closely is important because long tails can become tangled in future stitches or can show through to the right side of the canvas.

Using Even Tension. Keep your stitching tension consistent, with each stitch lying flat and even on the canvas. Pulling or yanking the yarn or floss causes the tension to be too tight, and you will be able to see through your project. Loose tension is caused by not pulling the yarn or floss firmly enough, and the yarn or floss will not lie flat on the canvas.

Ending Your Stitches. After you've completed all of the stitches of one color in an area, end your stitching by running your needle under several stitches on the back of the stitched piece. To keep the tails of the yarn or floss from showing through or becoming tangled in future stitches, trim the end of the yarn or floss close to the stitched piece.

JOINING PIECES

Straight Edges. The most common method of assembling stitched pieces is joining two or more pieces of canvas along a straight edge using overcast stitches. Place one piece on top of the other with right or wrong sides together. Make sure the edges being joined are even, then stitch the pieces together through all layers.

Shaded Areas. The shaded area is part of a chart that has colored shading on top of it. Shaded areas usually mean that all the stitches in that area are used to join pieces of canvas. Don't work stitches in a shaded area until your project instructions say you should.

Tacking. To tack pieces, run your needle under the backs of some stitches on one stitched piece to secure the yarn or floss. Then run your needle through the canvas or under the stitches on the piece to be tacked in place. The idea is to securely attach your pieces without your tacking stitches showing.

STITCH DIAGRAMS

Unless otherwise indicated, bring threaded needle up at 1 and all odd numbers and down at 2 and all even numbers.

TENT STITCH

This stitch is worked in horizontal and vertical rows over one intersection as shown in **Fig. 2**. Refer to **Fig. 3** to work the reversed tent stitch.

Fig. 2

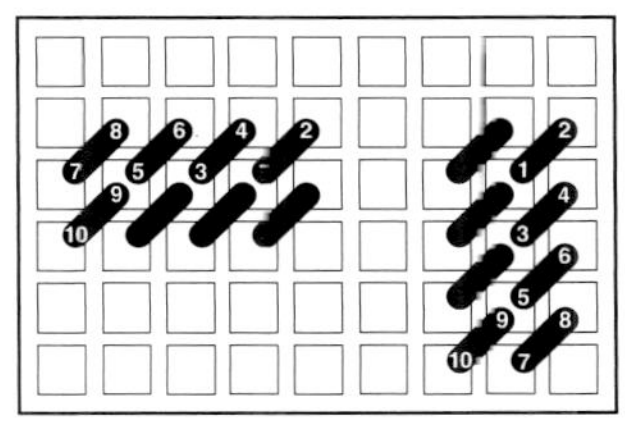

Fig. 3

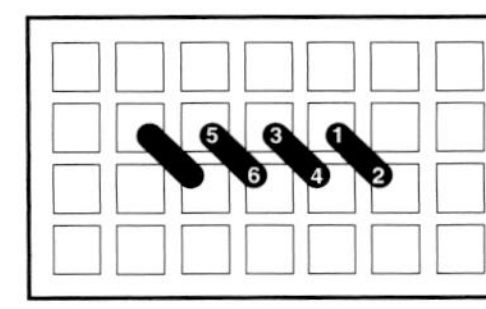

GOBELIN STITCH

This basic straight stitch is worked over two or more threads or intersections (**Fig. 4**). The number of threads or intersections may vary according to the chart.

Fig. 4

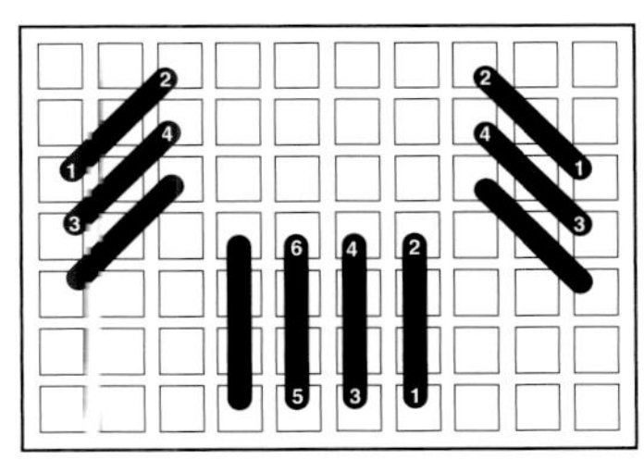

ALTERNATING SCOTCH STITCH

This Scotch stitch variation is worked over three or more threads forming alternating blocks as shown in **Fig. 5**.

Fig. 5

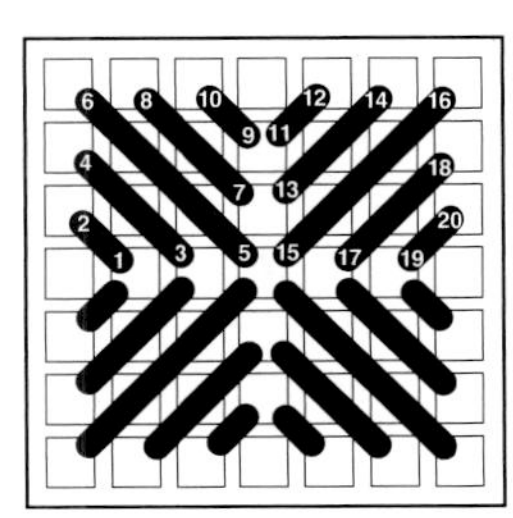

BACKSTITCH

This stitch is worked over completed stitches to outline or define (**Fig. 6**). It is sometimes worked over more than one thread.

Fig. 6

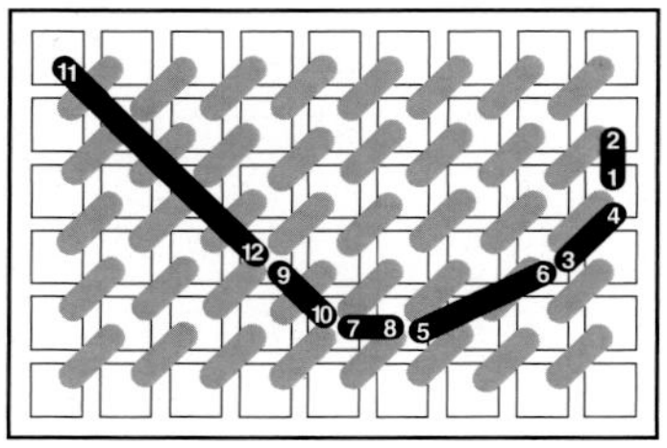

FRENCH KNOT

Come up at 1. Wrap yarn once around needle. Insert the needle at 2 and pull it through the canvas, holding the yarn until it must be released (**Fig. 7**).

Fig. 7

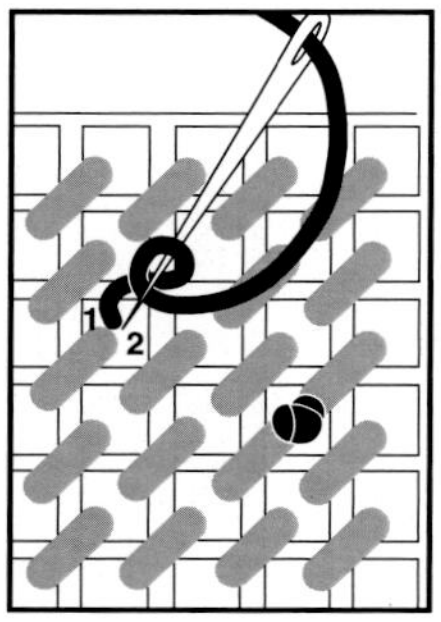

TURKEY LOOP STITCH

This stitch is composed of locked loops. Bring needle up through hole and back down through same hole, forming a loop on top of the canvas. A locking stitch is then made across the thread directly below or to either side of the loop as shown in **Fig. 8**.

Fig. 8

OVERCAST STITCH

This stitch covers the edge of the canvas and joins pieces of canvas (**Fig. 9**). It may be necessary to go through the same hole more than once to get even coverage on the edge, especially at the corners.

Fig. 9

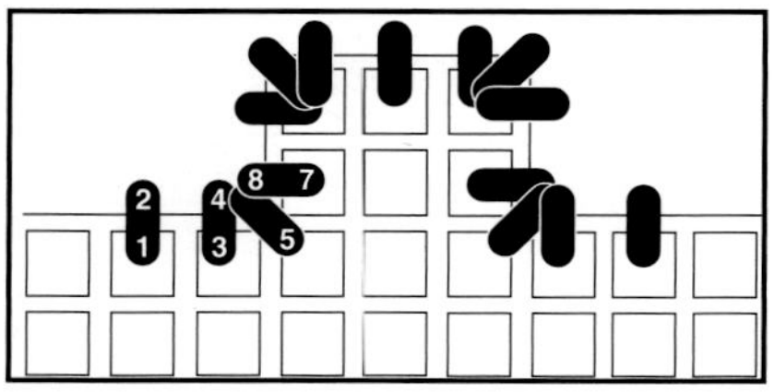

Pom-pom Diagrams

Diagram A

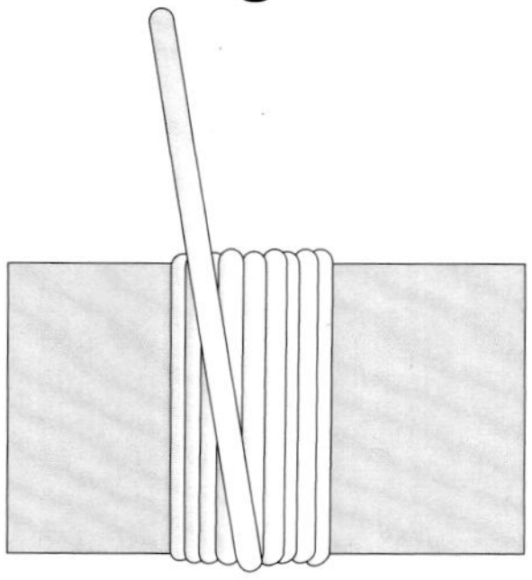

Diagram B

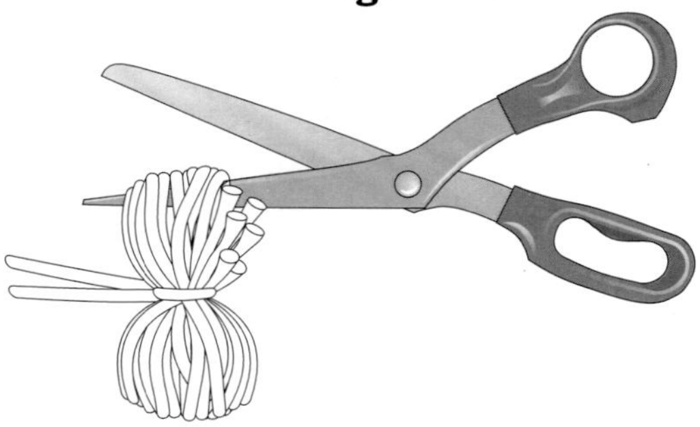